CULTIVATING ALL-AGE WORSHIP

Catherine Hammond

Contents

First edition 2000
Reprinted 2000

Published by
CPAS
Athena Drive
Tachbrook Park
WARWICK
CV34 6NG

Written by Catherine Hammond
Illustrated by Mark Burgess
Margin illustrations by Taffy Davies
Edited and designed by AD Publishing Services
Printed by Unigraph Printing Services

ISBN 1 902041 07 0

British Library Cataloguing-in-Publication Data
A catalogue record for this book is available from the British Library.

Church Pastoral Aid Society: Registered Charity No 1007820
A company limited by guarantee

Introduction

I am sometimes asked, 'Where do you get your ideas for all-age worship from?' Just to reply 'God', although it may be true, does not seem to me to be particularly helpful. Nor does it help to say, 'Oh, I don't do anything, they just come out of the blue.' While that is how it appears to be, in the depths of the blue are principles, people and procedures which have worked before, and mistakes to avoid repeating. So this is a book about growing ideas, and in particular about growing individual ideas for individual churches.

> *'And what is the use of a book,'*
> *thought Alice,*
> *'without pictures or conversation?'*
> (*Alice's Adventures in Wonderland*, Lewis Carroll)

The pictures in this book, both Mark's drawings and the word illustrations, are seeds from which new ideas can grow ('that wouldn't work, but we could…'). They were produced in an Anglican church with a supportive leadership, an unusual building and a fairly mobile congregation of people with a wide variety of church backgrounds. The ideas we have used can be taken, used or adapted as required. We hope that from them will sprout a whole new crop of ideas.

The book was designed both for people with responsibility for planning worship when all ages are present together and for those who think it might be a good idea to start thinking through that possibility. It could be used by:

- a minister to get a small group thinking
- a worship team to take stock of their work
- people looking for practical tips as they develop their own all-age worship programmes.

There are ten short chapters, most of which end with some activities to help you cultivate what is right for your church. There are sheets marked ℙ that can be photocopied on to paper or acetate to aid your discussions. One person could read through the text of a chapter and, using the action points, lead the group in discussion, prayer and planning. Alternatively each member of a group could read the chapter before the meeting and then share reactions and work through the activities. Any ideas or changes that arise from discussion will, of course, need to be developed within the constitutional framework of your church and with sensitivity to the other leaders and members of your congregation.

We have found that leading, planning and watching all-age worship grow is a wonderful, satisfying and risky privilege. Our hope is that this book will encourage more ideas to germinate that are ideally suited to the terrain and climate of other churches.

The workbook begins with a look at the principles underlying all-age worship and moves on to suggest how different churches can work this out in ways appropriate to them. There are practical tips in chapter 6, ideas for the summer in chapter 9 and thoughts on being a community of all ages in chapter 10.

To start off the cultivation, we begin with the roots.

PRINCIPLES OF CULTIVATION

CHAPTER 1

Principles to grow from

Fifteen minutes past ten and I find myself wrestling with the question: 'Why have we planned a service with so much nerve-wracking involvement? Why not stick to the safety of a book?' An hour later and I have usually found out the answer.

Bringing all ages together and opening windows on to God is a privilege. It is also a risky business – we risk embarking on something that may not work; we risk criticism and we risk meeting God together in an unexpected way. But it is also exciting – an opportunity to help bring the family of God, in all its diversity, into the arms of almighty God.

So, where do we begin a re-think, a first shot or a trial run? Why not forget thinking about the next service for a while and look for some principles from which to start.

All ages?

You also, like living stones,
are being built into a spiritual house
to be a holy priesthood,
offering spiritual sacrifices acceptable to
* God through Jesus Christ.*
(1 Peter 2:5)

When I picture the spiritual house that Peter writes about I imagine it built with dry stone walls rather like those found in many parts of the British Isles: different sized pieces of rock with no cement holding them together but carefully arranged so that the wall can stand for years. Some of the stones have had their difficult corners and edges knocked off with a hammer so that they can fit next to their neighbours.

The church is composed of members with many differences, but somehow we all fit together. Sometimes we need chipping and shaping before we can fit with each other and then, as a community, we are enabled to offer spiritual sacrifices acceptable to God through Christ Jesus. Our worship comes out of our corporate life together. This does not, of course, mean that we wait until we feel that our life as a community is right before we can start worshipping – we would never begin! But what is possible and appropriate in worship will change as our life as a church develops.

God also speaks of the church in other collective images: a holy nation, a royal priesthood, the household of God, a family. Worshipping together helps make the reality of our calling clear to us. In sharing worship, we find we are closer to each other. In moving closer to each other, we come closer to God.

Being a church for all ages does not mean that we do everything together. It does, I think, mean that we all move towards treating each other as fellow members of the household of God, regardless of age. Conversation, understanding and support will then become natural across generations.

Jesus communicated with many different people on an individual basis. Flicking through the beginning of John's Gospel we find him talking to:

- an ascetic man with a prophetic gift
- fishermen
- servants at a wedding celebration
- temple traders
- a well-educated Jewish leader
- a Samaritan woman
- a boy with a picnic.

In each case, he was 'himself' with that person: he did not ignore or patronize any of them, but accepted their personality and responded appropriately. We, too, can come as we are with our own personalities and our own histories, but we come together as a church with one faith and one Lord.

Services for all-age worship provide opportunities for the church as a whole to:

- respond together to God's love and revelation of himself
- behave as God's household or a spiritual building
- grow in the understanding that although its members have different needs and gifts, they have one Lord.

In practice, worshipping with all ages together:

- reminds us that in our relationship with God we are all learning and growing
- allows children to see that there will always be a place for them in the church and in God's love
- allows all ages (including the elderly) to make valuable contributions
- lets adults learn from the wonder and imagination, the trust and desire for action that children bring and which adults themselves may have lost.

Worship

Two thousand years ago some people set out specifically to worship a young Jewish king. When they reached Bethlehem they recognized in Jesus the king they had been searching for. *'They bowed down and worshipped him. Then they opened their treasures and presented him with gifts'* (Matthew 2:11).

CHAPTER 1

In that story the wise men recognized Jesus, showed their allegiance to him and presented their gifts. As we plan to lead others in worship, we need to remember that they will need:

● the opportunity to reflect on or learn something of God so that they may respond to him
● the opportunity to offer their allegiance, their loyalty and their service
● the chance to give.

In our services we need to provide times for each of the above. So planning worship is about opening windows – providing opportunities for our congregation to receive from God and to respond to him together. The psalmist in Psalm 95 said:

Come, let us sing for joy to the Lord…
for the Lord is the great God, the great King above all gods…
Come, let us bow down in worship, let us kneel before the Lord our Maker…
(Psalm 95:1,3,6)

The psalmist's knowledge of God led to an expression in song of praise and thanksgiving and an action symbolic of his desire to serve God.

ACTION

AIM: To consider what it means to be a worshipping community

1. Look up the following verses and think through what this particular picture of the church says to you. Share your results.

Chosen people	1 Peter 2:9,10
Holy nation	1 Peter 2:9,10
Fellow citizens	Ephesians 2:19-22
Members of God's household	Ephesians 2:19-22
Living stones in a spiritual house	1 Peter 2:4,5
Children of God	Galatians 3:26
Body	1 Corinthians 12:12-14

2. In planning worship, opportunities need to be provided for the congregation to:

● reflect on or increase their knowledge of God
● offer to God their service
● respond to God by giving.

In Psalm 116 the psalmist worships God. On a copy (see Worksheet A, page 7) highlight the points where the psalmist:

● shows his knowledge of God
● offers to God his allegiance
● speaks of giving to God.

Psalm 116

I love the Lord, for he heard my voice;
he heard my cry for mercy.
Because he turned his ear to me,
I will call on him as long as I live.
The cords of death entangled me,
the anguish of the grave came upon me;
I was overcome by trouble and sorrow.
Then I called on the name of the Lord:
'O Lord, save me!'

The Lord is gracious and righteous;
our God is full of compassion.
The Lord protects the simple-hearted;
when I was in great need, he saved me.

Be at rest once more, O my soul,
for the Lord has been good to you.

For you, O Lord, have delivered my soul from death,
my eyes from tears,
my feet from stumbling,
that I may walk before the Lord
in the land of the living.
I believed; therefore I said,
'I am greatly afflicted.'
And in my dismay I said,
'All men are liars.'

How can I repay the Lord
for all his goodness to me?
I will lift up the cup of salvation
and call on the name of the Lord.
I will fulfil my vows to the Lord
in the presence of all his people.

Precious in the sight of the Lord
is the death of his saints.

O Lord, truly I am your servant;
I am your servant, the son of your maidservant;
you have freed me from my chains.

I will sacrifice a thank-offering to you
and call on the name of the Lord.
I will fulfil my vows to the Lord
in the presence of all his people,
in the courts of the house of the Lord –
in your midst, O Jerusalem.

Praise the Lord.

CHAPTER 2

Roots

If all-age worship services were plants, they would grow and develop, changing shape, sometimes flowering, sometimes not. They would vary from place to place depending on the local environment and care, but they would be dependent on God for growth. They would also have roots from which they grow (and which remain if the leaves are pruned or cut).

The roots are the principles from which creative acts of worship can grow. Drama, prayer, singing, activity… these are the things that people see – the leaves and flowers of services. But supporting them and guiding their growth are the roots, the principles on which worship has been planned.

Take, for example, the set of roots shown at the foot of this page. These roots have proved to be very creative but have also guided the plant in its growth. Take away the God-centred root and you are left with merely Christian entertainment. If you forget that God deals with individual churches then you will produce sickly clones of other more vibrant plants. If you fail to consider that all ages are together then you will alienate groups or individuals. Being sure of your roots is a guide in

planning and evaluating, and a help in coping with criticism. But what does it mean in practice, and how does a plant grow from this set of roots?

The God-centred root

God must be the focus of our worship. We have come together not as a club but as a church responding to God. So we come not to get something for ourselves, but to appreciate together something of God's nature, which will then evoke a response in us.

Sometimes we have wrong expectations of services, like the child who, after going to a few parties, knows the form and, to the horror of her mother, expects to go home with a party bag. The party invitation has been turned into a chance to 'get' rather than to honour the birthday child. Comments like 'I don't really like all-age worship – I don't get anything out of the services' reveal this sort of attitude.

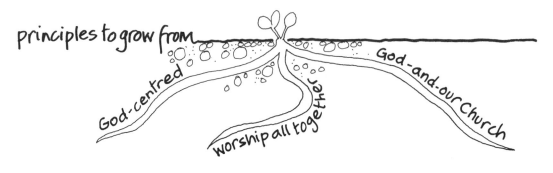

principles to grow from

God-centred   God-and-our Church

worship all together

8

Within the framework of our services there should be opportunity for God to speak through his word, to touch our lives by his Spirit or meet us in the sacrament, and then space for some response in words, actions, songs, life-changing dedication. So together, we should have an opportunity to worship – to give God his worth, expressing and valuing his character.

You are worthy, our Lord and God,
to receive glory and honour and power,
for you created all things,
and by your will they were created and
have their being.
(Revelation 4:11)

In planning our worship we always need to remember its God-centred focus. How can we ensure that our planning is God-centred?

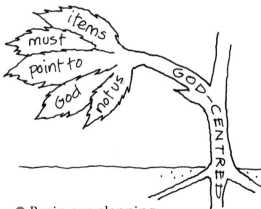

- Begin our planning by prayer and Bible reading.
- Ask what God wants from this service.
- Avoid items that are there solely because the children are doing it (or any other group).
- Ask, 'Does what we are planning to do fit within our whole understanding of God's character, or is it misleading?' (e.g. Does our interpretation of 'God is love' make him look soppy and sentimental?)

The God-and-our-church root

What is your church like? What are the possibilities and limitations, already provided in the congregation, the building and its history? How does all-age worship fit within the whole worship programme?

People

In many churches the members are mobile, staying for a few years and then moving on. Congregations like these are ever-changing kaleidoscopes of gifts, put together in different ways for the good of God's church.

History

What are the treasures of your tradition? What could be used in a new way or a new setting that will light up both your history and the current service? Are there core elements you must include in your all-age worship – spoken words, symbolic actions, sacraments?

Buildings

Can you use the spaces and surfaces within the building in new ways? For example:

- walls, pillars, ceilings could be used for projecting overheads or for hanging artwork
- floor space could be used for maps, giant books, models and drama
- the building may provide scope for people to move from one part to another.

CHAPTER 2

Programmes

Where is your church now in its journey with God? How are you responding to recent joys, sadnesses, problems and successes? What are you learning from God now? There need to be good links between the church staff and the all-age worship planning co-ordinator if all-age worship is to become part of the ongoing learning and worship of the church, complementing other services and the work done in age-related groups. Some of the music, liturgy and insights used by the church at other times can be incorporated into the all-age services so that links and understanding are developed from shared material.

ACTION

AIM: To consider the opportunities available within your own church.

It would be best to do this exercise in the building that you worship in.

1. Discuss what experiences have developed your church's walk with God recently, e.g. teaching, long-term love and service of staff or congregation, changes in staff, challenging projects, tragedies, changes in the local environment...

   Reflect individually on the question: 'What do you think God is teaching my church now?' Share any insights.

2. Walk round your church building together then use Worksheet B (on page 11) to consider the resources and gifts available in your church. Write in any ideas on the leaves. Your ideas may include items from the tradition and style of worship of your church, the spiritual and natural gifts of your congregation and the resources that your building offers.

3. Finally, add any thoughts from Question 1 to the 'our journey with God' leaf.

What possibilities do you see in your church for each of the resources/gifts marked?

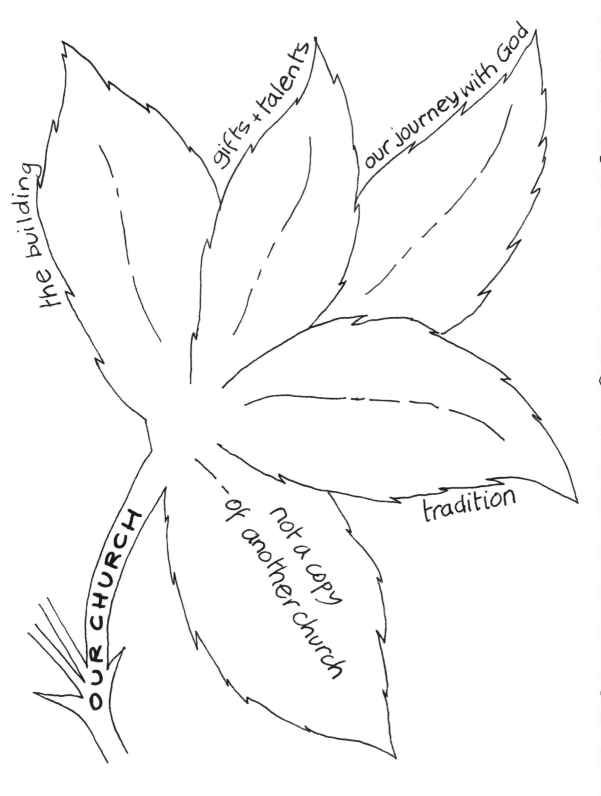

the building

gifts + talents

our journey with God

OUR CHURCH

not a copy of another church

tradition

The third root

The third root, the 'worship-all-together' root, takes into account that we are planning for all ages together. This root sends out two shoots which it may be helpful to consider separately:

● different age groups have different characteristics
● in spite of these differences, the church has gathered to worship all together.

To bear both in mind means that we need to know something of what children, young people and adults are like.

Characteristics of different ages

Physically, mentally, spiritually, socially and emotionally we change, as we grow older. Think of age-related groups in our society:

● crèche
● toddler groups
● play groups
● infants
● juniors
● secondary school pupils
● young adults
● middle aged
● early retired
● frail elderly

The concentration span, desire to be on the move, understanding of abstract ideas, physical ability and so on change as people grow older.

Faith, too, develops. If we consider faith to be composed of believing, trusting and doing (see *Children Finding Faith* by Francis Bridger) then

the balance between those three elements changes as we grow older.

For the **youngest children**, babies, toddlers and those at infant school, trust is all-important.

As intellectual and physical abilities develop, the capacity for a believing-faith and a doing-faith grows. **Junior children** have an enormous interest and curiosity in the world and this includes what people believe. This intellectual belief will, however, be in very concrete terms; abstract ideas cannot be handled at this age. Being by now very physically active, '*doing* their faith' becomes important.

Secondary school pupils embark on the difficult process of finding their identity. Their friendship groups become more important than the influences provided by school, family or other social structures, so it is a time for challenging authority and being dominated by their feelings. Their faith will be very much influenced by the faith of their friends.

Moving into **adulthood** may involve further growth in faith as people search for truth that will ring true for them and on which they can then base their lives.

These stages and the ages suggested may not always correspond – growth in faith may stop and start at any point – but they are a useful starting place for our thinking. A consideration of the broad differences between age groups will enable leaders to plan so that people are not excluded unnecessarily and their gifts can be used for the benefit of all. There are several factors that it is helpful to consider:

- *physical considerations* such as adjusting the length of time a group composed of all ages can be expected to stand or sit still
- *intellectual considerations* – using non-abstract but not babyish language
- *spiritual considerations* – ensuring that the way the building is used and the style of leadership given make the church a safe place in which trust can grow and questioning is accepted.

In broad terms, a shoot from this root might look like this:

Each of these characteristics can be taken into account in the planning of a service without directing it solely at that particular age group. Here are some examples:

Visuals

If people particularly need something visual to hold their attention, this can be introduced at the same time as words that may appeal to those with an intellectual side to their faith. For example, the story of Ruth was retold over several weeks with the aid of nearly life-size cardboard cut-outs. They were moved from place to place as the story progressed, by children standing behind them. This simple device was enough to capture the interest of everyone.

Quiet

After twenty minutes of frantic activity constructing olive trees in the church hall, the congregation sat in silence looking at simple sleeping figures beside a candle representing Jesus. It was a moment of silence and meditation, but the scene that had been prepared helped those who would not normally want to be

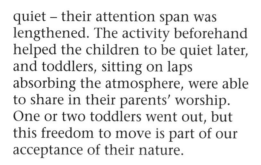

quiet – their attention span was lengthened. The activity beforehand helped the children to be quiet later, and toddlers, sitting on laps absorbing the atmosphere, were able to share in their parents' worship. One or two toddlers went out, but this freedom to move is part of our acceptance of their nature.

Facing questions

The faith of young people grows as they question the faith they have been brought up in or see in others. To be accepted as they wrestle with the big questions of life is important. Living as a Christian is not easy; sometimes we have to hold our problems and pains next to our faith, not denying either. We have to recognize that we have no string of simple answers.

The title 'I believe in God the Father, who made the world' looked like a straightforward subject for a service. As we met to plan the service, we soon realized that not only had a recent service already taken a straight look at God our Creator, but there was also a danger of making too simple a statement. God made the world and it was good; yet all around the pain, disaster and illness shrieks the opposite. It was some time before we got to the point where we could say that the central theme of the service would be to show that the God who created the world cares for it always. From that sprang a drama involving a working machine and its inventor and maintenance man (one and the same). We struggled to make the machine work and doubted the wisdom of putting in so much effort,

but in the end it was an unforgettable approach to some of life's questions. Looking back it was all worthwhile.

In practice, visual and active elements introduced with children in mind often help adults to learn and to respond to God. Familiar stories have a new impact, new realizations dawn and opportunities to respond actively touch people deeply.

Worshipping all together

Differences do not mean that each age group has to be considered in turn, so that by the end of the service everyone has had something suited to them. To do that is to miss the opportunity of offering to God a united act of worship.

In the examples already used, people of different ages were able to participate because the item could be taken at different levels.

A service on the loving care of God began with a sketch of a mother and a 'toddler' (all 6'3" of him!) in a shopping trolley. Despite the obvious mishaps that occurred as the mother took her wilful child armed with a French stick round the supermarket, the mother's love continued enough for her to bring her offspring home where she went on caring for him. Among the responses were:

- surprise
- laughter
- enjoyment
- anticipation
- realization of the mother's love

- realization that God's love is greater
- appreciation that God's love goes on and on and copes with us.

People of all ages could find a rung of response on which to stand.

It can be helpful to check back through a service plan to see if an age group's needs are being met. But if you feel they are missing out, don't just insert a specific item designed for that age group; adjust what is already there so that it draws that age group into the worship of the whole church. Traditionally, groups within churches have often been invited to contribute something for the whole church – to lead the prayers, to lead a time of worship, to sing at a carol service… Leading all-age worship gives us the opportunity to 'mix' people by asking them to work on something together. It can be another step in helping people to get to know each other and so help the church as a whole make its offering to God.

Age is not the only differentiating factor within a congregation. A young couple with a two-year-old may well feel differently from a single person of the same age, or from a person for whom family life has been mostly painful. At every age there will be differences produced by experience of the world and of God and by the understanding of themselves as individuals and as a member of the church. Being aware

of the members of the congregation will give us a greater sensitivity in the use of material and a greater vision of God's kingdom.

One of the joys of being involved in worship with all ages is to discover that someone has been unexpectedly touched by the service. It might have been the sudden realization for an adult, as they laid their footprints next to ones representing the footsteps of Jesus, that when they go into the outside world, God is already there. Or it might have been a sense of unexpected wonder as children revealed paper planets and stars and the universe was described. It is a good thing for those planning all-age worship to look back and review recent services, to see where there have been unexpected joys – or problems.

So now, with roots established, the planning can begin.

ACTION

AIM: To consider how services can be designed so that different ages are given the opportunity to worship together.

1. Using copies of Worksheet C, fill in individual answers then share your ideas.

2. Discuss and complete Worksheet D together. File this sheet and set a date to review it.

WORKSHEET C

Which characteristics would you link with which age group?

Likes quiet and meditation

Small

Restless when still

Questioning

Cannot grasp abstract ideas

Visual items help keep their attention

Very short attention span

Has faith with an intellectual component

Likes to be part of a group

Has faith based on the faith of others

Cannot read easily

Now look again at the characteristics and suggest ways in which they can be used positively in a service.

**Colour the leaves to show which areas
in your church need to be addressed**

- immediately
- in the next year
- in the next five years.

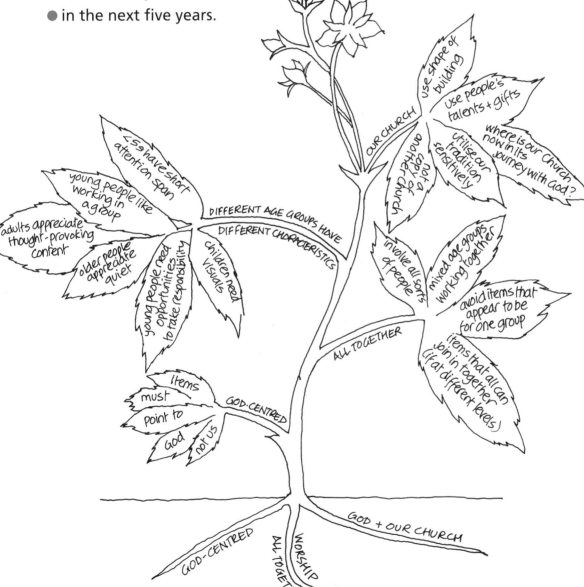

PRACTICAL CULTIVATION

CHAPTER 4

The blank page

Imagine you are planning an all-age service, alone or with your planning group. You sit with pen poised in front of a blank sheet of paper. There is just the date of the next service at the top of the page and perhaps a title – the next subject in your church's teaching programme or the relevant readings from the Lectionary. Looking over your shoulder are people and items waiting to see if they are going to be included. Some may always appear – music, prayer, Scripture or specific pieces of liturgy (e.g. the Lord's Prayer or an agreed Service of the Word or Eucharistic Service). Others are not so sure that they will be needed – drama, the dance group, straight Bible readings, antiphonal psalms, children's art… Peering between the other heads are the ideas you have picked up from schools, theatre, exhibitions and the knowledge of where your church is at the moment in its walk with God. And further back, where you are barely aware of them, are the groups and skills you have not used before in these services and the ideas you have not thought of yet. Looking round at all the faces and turning back to the paper, you wonder how to make a start on the right list.

We are creative people because we are made in the image of our Creator God. Planning worship is an opportunity to use that creativity, as we look for the best ways to open windows on to God. In this creative process there is no foolproof recipe for success in choosing what to include. Churches and planners are all different, and God – who is the master of revelation – will not be pinned down by his creation.

Ideas for worship seem to have a lot in common with poems and hums.

'But it isn't easy,' (said Winnie the Pooh) *'because poetry and hums aren't things which you get, they're things that get you. And all you can do is go where they can find you.'*
(*The House at Pooh Corner*, A A Milne)

Here are some things that may help us to be in the 'right' place where ideas for worship can be found:

- intending to listen – to God and to each other
- working with a group
- finding one point and aiming for it
- being prepared not to have come up with a final order of service at the end of every meeting – and to be ready to change it.

Listening

The ways God speaks to us in the context of a service are not always the obvious ones. For example, sunlight on flowers, people's faces, silence, music without words… In

planning worship, the aim is to create opportunities for our congregation to communicate with God – both in speaking and in listening. So listening to God must have a key role in our planning. If we meet as a planning group we need to come with:

- an awareness of anything God has shown us recently
- a readiness to listen to each other
- a willingness to share our ideas and not have them accepted
- an acknowledgement that we need God's direction, wisdom and grace.

In practice that may mean: prayer, Bible reading, reading from other books, silence, talk, laughter, coffee and cake, doodles and crossings out, more prayer...

Working with a group

What makes a good group? A really good group is made up of people who love God and want to learn more of him, and who have a vision for drawing people together for worship. They may also bring with them skills – music, drama, theological knowledge, ability to create a flowing order of service, understanding of young people, dance, drawing... Looking first for love and vision does not devalue those talents but creates the right contexts for them to be used. Sometimes we need to look for people with particular skills, but we need also to make sure that they have, or can catch, the vision of the whole. I have worked with some

extremely talented people, without whom a lot of the services we have planned would not have been possible, but they have offered their gifts to help the church worship as a whole rather than simply promote their own areas of expertise or interest.

There are different kinds of gifts, but the same Spirit.
There are different kinds of service, but the same Lord.
There are different kinds of working, but the same God works all of them in all men.
Now to each one the manifestation of the Spirit is given for the common good.
(1 Corinthians 12:4-7)

A group shares the laughter, pain and work and helps sort out the daft but good idea from the ideas that are not right for this time. It should be a source of strength and able to cope with the mistakes that will be made, while at the same time holding on to the vision. It will work best in an environment of trust so a group needs to make the effort to build links with the rest of the church; not only through involving other people, but also by listening to their comments and criticism and by being ready to change if necessary. What is possible and effective depends on the willingness of others to participate, to pray and to encourage. 'Others' includes both the church leadership or staff and people from the congregation at large. Without the support of the leadership, all-age worship becomes an interesting off-shoot and not part of the whole developing church.

CHAPTER 4

One possibility for support is to set up a group composed of the main leaders/co-ordinators of children's work, youthwork and all-age worship, along with someone whose role is to encourage. The 'encourager' is to take an interest, arrange occasional meetings and provide (in whatever ways seem appropriate) an atmosphere of trust. It is particularly helpful to receive this personal care from outside those working with children and young people, and from outside the leadership team.

The person who says 'thank you' and means it, or who takes an interest in the concerns of someone twenty years younger or older, helps more than they can imagine.

Getting to the point

Sometimes I have tried to see what should have been achieved by the end of a meeting, especially after a session when we don't appear to have arrived anywhere. There doesn't seem to be a set pattern, but this perhaps should not surprise us since God is a master of surprises. Some different patterns have emerged as a result of our planning meetings, for example:

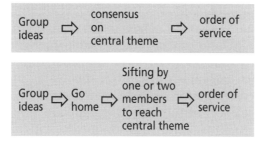

| Group with one idea | ⇨ | Complete order of service |

These patterns suggest that somewhere in the process a central theme is always agreed. This is not to limit what God may say in the service but it helps make the service flow and be understood by a variety of ages. If we are not clear where we are going it is easy to go round in circles!

There will, of course, be exceptions. Harvest seems to come with several points already built in, but wrestling with them will help sort out the right theme for that particular time. One Pentecost we spent the whole meeting discussing what was important in the Pentecost story for our church that year. By the end of the meeting we had no order of service. At times like this, it is easy to feel a sense of despair and failure – 'perhaps it's time to quit'. But the service plan that came to mind in the following week could not have been reached without all that background thinking.

It is possible to start from a series of blocks and fill in the gaps. But beginning with a blank page and an awareness of all the possibilities forces you to listen more to God – and it makes you more creative.

The next step is to make the service flow from one item to the next with the minimum of fuss.

ACTION

AIM: To consider what helps us worship God together and to get beyond the blank planning page.

1. Individually, list all the ways that have helped you learn of God and worship him within a church service.

Now share your lists with the group, remembering that each list will be very special to its writer as it recalls some of their encounters with God.

2. Look at the items listed round the border of Worksheet E, then, using your own lists, add anything that you feel is missing.

3. For your next service, using copies of the sheet produced in Question 2 above, work through the following steps:

- Pray that you will be good listeners.
- Read a relevant Bible passage.
- Think and talk, trying to arrive at one central theme – write it in.
- Discuss how that can best be conveyed to the congregation, and what would help them respond.
- Choose the items from the border of the sheet that could be included.

If you have no service to prepare, take Acts 2 and, using the steps above, plan a service for Pentecost.

Tackling the blank page

banners

intercessions

statements of belief

dramatic reading

talking

prayers of praise

silence

models

reading

dance

action

Date _____

Subject _____

_____

Central theme _____

_____

drama to make a point

songs

music

pictures

OHP slides

confession

traditional hymns

antiphonal/choral reading

Scripture in drama

communion

Flow and fine tuning

I have a friend who composes and arranges music. Somehow in her work there is balance and flow, beginnings and endings. This is vastly different from the rawness of the new recorder player who may play the right notes in the right sequence but cannot generate continuity or feeling. Like orchestral music, orders of service need beginnings and endings, balance and movement. Yet we have already seen that the attention span of younger children is not long, and as a result we have probably included a number of short items in our service, making achieving a sense of flow more difficult. Similarly, by looking for input from different people, using their gifts, we may end up with a disjointed programme. So how can we help the list of items become a flowing order of service, giving opportunity for all to worship God together?

Sequence

The right order is often fairly obvious as we consider the whole message of the service. It's a sort of 'converse' Cheshire-Cat principle:

'Would you tell me, please, which way I ought to go from here?' (said Alice)
'That depends a good deal on where you want to get to,' said the Cat.
'I don't much care where –' said Alice.
'Then it doesn't matter which way you go,' said the Cat.
(*Alice's Adventures in Wonderland,* Lewis Carroll)

Behind the list of components, there needs to be a progression in our thoughts as we walk together before God. This allows people to move with the flow of the service, without the confusion and uneasiness that might limit their ability to understand or respond.

Take, for example, the account of Peter, after the resurrection, meeting Jesus on the beach (John 21).

Our main point might be:

Peter was given a new start based on the fact that Jesus loved him and he loved Jesus.

The underlying progression could then be:

Failure ➔ meeting Jesus ➔ new start ➔ new responsibility

And for us the flow in a service might be:

Recognition of failure

Confession
⬇
Absolution
⬇
Appreciation of new start
⬇
Prayer for those taking on responsibilities
⬇
Our own recommitment

The items we have already thought about can then be woven into that developing stream. For example:

Welcome and Easter song
⬇
Drama involving museum worker who drops valuable pots but is given new job at the museum

Confession, space to think, and absolution
↓
Reading and pictures of Peter
↓
Explanation comparing the drama with Peter and relating it to us
↓
Prayer for ourselves and others and our responsibilities
↓
Song of commitment

Into this flow other songs and activities would be inserted.

The order of songs and the feelings they will engender are important. There needs to be a progression so that people are not asked to lurch from one emotion to another.

As we check the sequence we will see if too many similar items follow each other. Sometimes we may need to make changes, even last-minute ones. For example, after seeing a dramatic retelling of the life of Joseph for the first time before a service, we realized that the amount of humour and activity in it could not be followed by the serious item we had planned. Instead, the fairly lively song scheduled for later was moved earlier, giving people the opportunity to digest the drama and be involved in activity. In the event, this reordering worked much better than the original plan would have done.

The final details:
Service leaders

If we listen to a piece of orchestral music, the conductor is not continuously the focus of our attention. Similarly, the service leader should be big enough to be seen pointing to God, but small enough to be seen past.

The congregation needs to feel that the leader is sufficiently in control for them to be free to worship God. Linking pieces together may not, in fact, take many words, so leaders need to be people who say only what is necessary to bring in the different items but who say it with a warmth that puts people at ease and a clear vision of where the service is going. A leader needs to be someone who offers their best, with an honesty in their relationship with God and with the congregation. The cost of that is to make them horribly vulnerable, but the gain is to be part of a communication process with God. On Sunday mornings this all

seems to be too much to ask. I wake wondering why I am about to be in this position. Perhaps a lack of self-confidence is a good thing, since all I can do is to trust God and go for it. Mistakes are not disasters; they may even give the congregation the confidence needed to perform their part. A church that allows people to fail without disgrace offers its leaders and itself the opportunity to learn and grow.

Other people

Sharing in leading a service gives opportunities for people's gifts to be used, recognized and developed. We need to be sensitive in choosing the right number of people to be involved. Too many voices can be confusing and time consuming; too few may be monotonous. These people need a clear idea of where the service is going, what is required of them and when. They need to be confident that any practical details in what they are doing have been taken care of – can they be seen, heard, etc? It is the responsibility of the planners to ensure that what is offered by others is put in the best setting. If you look at the walls of a primary school, you will see that the children's work has been carefully mounted and arranged. That same care needs to be given to our children and adults so that their contributions are known to be valued, and they see that the church is trying to offer its best to God. Taking time to think about the details is time well spent.

Starting

Starting out on the right foot is important. Alienate people at the beginning and it will be difficult to draw them in again later. 'How many more songs are there going to be?' may be the whisper of a younger worshipper if we pick the wrong song to start with. It is good to develop a reservoir of known songs shared by children and adults so that the response becomes, 'O good, I know this one.' I have heard both comments on different occasions. When choosing an activity that requires participation, we may choose one that will draw people in or one that is too demanding and loses them. Start with too much talk and nothing visual, and you can see children resigning themselves to a morning's boredom.

In fact, the congregation have started before the start. What are they doing or thinking about when they come in? Do they greet the people around them, listen to the music, join in with the songs, or sit and watch? If we want people to come in with a sense of anticipation, we need to help them by providing something that will capture their interest.

In a service about the ongoing love of God we looped the church with 100m of yellow florist's ribbon. It was obvious that it was there, although in some places it disappeared from view. I hope that it generated such thoughts as 'I wonder what it is there for?' and 'What's going to happen?' Adults often need that sort of help to enable them to share a sense of expectation with small children in worship. The opening remarks of that service drew attention to the ribbon, but the answers came much later with the realization that the loop,

CHAPTER 5

although not always visible, was in fact continuous.

And finally...

Check the balance between:

- listening activities and responses
- standing and sitting
- movement and stillness
- talk and action.

If you think you need more involvement, consider chapter 7. For practical tips, look at the next chapter.

After that, offer what has been prepared and all those who will take part to God, who alone can put wings on our worship.

ACTION

AIM: To ensure that a proposed service flows.

1. Take either the list of items for a proposed order of service or the list you have made for Question 3 of the action page of the last chapter. Turn the list into a flow chart by adding arrows from one to another.

2. Will the order provide people with a progression of thought, feeling, atmosphere, response?

3. What, if anything, needs to be said at each arrow?

4. Highlight the times when the congregation is asked to stand or move, and consider whether they have sat for too long.

Tips for cultivation

With your planning page no longer blank, there still remains a gap between it and a fully-grown service. Here are some practical tips that may be useful in your situation.

Finding visuals

- Mull over the point you are hoping to make or the story you want to tell. See if any images spring to mind. Beware of producing a memorable visual image that does not remind the congregation of the right point.
- Look at the available space – floor, walls, pillars…
- What will everyone be able to see?
- Consider using maps, books, jigsaws, scenery – houses, trees, figures
- Can visual clues be used to arouse curiosity and then be built on as the service or talk develops?
- Large drawings can be made by photocopying a small source on to acetate and using an overhead projector to blow it up to the right size on a drawing surface. Then draw round the image. If it is then coloured and cut out, it helps to leave a white edge around it; this makes it stand out from its surroundings.
- Check back – is this particular visual image the lasting impression you want to leave with the congregation?

Orders of service

Orders of service (and similar leaflets) can be used to:

- enable the congregation to join in better
- help promote a sense of expectancy
- provide something that will help people to continue their thoughts at home
- avoid using a service book that may appear daunting
- provide illustrations that will help non-readers cope with set services that contain a lot of words e.g. Baptism, Holy Communion. (Check the copyright rules to ensure that permission for copying is available.)

Remembering that not everyone is an accomplished reader:

- words are best in a clear font that is not too small
- drawings are helpful – clipart is readily available
- the whole leaflet/card can look interesting and attractive
- do not use unnecessary words.

As well as orders of services there are all sorts of other possibilities – cards that can be refolded to make a new point, cards with pieces to slot in or stick on, cards to offer as a symbol of our gift to God, cards to take away as a reminder of his gift to us, cards good enough to keep as a reminder of what was learnt…

Overhead projectors

Projectors are useful to:

- make a point
- tell a story
- accompany a Bible reading
- illustrate the people and places in prayers.

They can show:

- drawings
- 'paintings' – using washable pens the colours can be shaded together with water and a cotton bud or tissue
- pictures that are built up with overlays
- silhouettes – paper shapes can be cut out and stuck to the acetate
- photocopies of pictures, drawings, photos
- words – but make sure that the letters are large enough and the gap between lines is bigger than you would use in normal writing.

Acetates look best within a frame, which gives the added bonus of space to write cues on. They can project on to the walls and ceiling as well as on to a screen. To shine a picture high up on the wall the picture can be made within a frame shaped as in the drawing. This allows for the distortion that occurs when the image is projected at a large angle from the horizontal. To discover the right-shaped frame, put the projector in position and, with the light on, place card strips to mark the four edges of the frame. Adjust them until you get the projected frame that you want. Tape the strips together. Mark

the position of the projector on the floor so that the final drawing is shown from the right place.

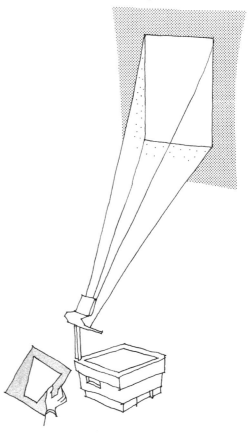

Talks

- Consider what really needs to be said. Much of what could be said may have already been covered in other ways.
- Often it is more effective to use bite-size talks through the service as the theme develops, rather than to aim to put it all into one talk.
- Link the spoken word to visuals or to what people have already done, seen or heard.
- Stories are memorable and involve people by engaging their imagination.

Prayers

- Make sure that whoever is leading the prayers knows what is expected of them.
- A few short prayers are usually better than a long continuous one.
- Use a form that is easy to follow and makes it easy for people to know when to say, 'Amen.' For example:

Dear	Loving God
You are	You have set us in the wonderful world of your creating
Please	Help us to live as responsible members of it, caring for each other and living wisely and lovingly
Because	So that we may please you, who in wisdom, made us all.
Yours sincerely	Through Jesus Christ our Lord. Amen.

- Responsive prayers using a repeated phrase allow everyone to join in whether they can read or not.
- Prayers can be made silently, while looking at pictures, or to music.
- Prayers can be written or drawn by the congregation as well as said or thought.

Reading

- Setting the scene helps – there is a culture gap between the people of AD2000 and those whose lives are described in the Bible.
- Consider using more than one voice, or responsive readings or choral readings.
- Illustrate the reading with OHP pictures or moveable cardboard figures or mime.
- Ensure that readers can be heard – practise if necessary.

Songs

- Work with whoever normally is responsible for music either from the start in a planning group or closely after the service outline has been planned.
- Choose songs that fit within the service as a whole, rather than chosen as a separate entity.
- Check that the words of songs and the images they convey are reasonably easy to understand.
- People of all ages need to be able to sing any chosen song with integrity.
- If it is too long or the tune is boring children will switch off.
- Consider the balance of type of music and the flow of the service.
- Consider the possibility of using young musicians with the usual music group, and letting the very young use shakers.
- Standing up and singing for a long time can be uncomfortable for the elderly, the pregnant, the young adolescent whose voice is breaking, and anyone who is tired.

Writing your own drama

- It helps if the writer can be involved from the start in the planning of the service; this gives them a feel for the service as a whole and they will be in tune with the central theme.
- Any writing needs to take into account what is possible within the available space. For example:
  - Note where actors can be seen.
    - Can they sit down and still be seen? If not, all action must be standing up.
    - Can they be seen when they are standing? If not, then the drama must take the form of a dialogue with the expression and emphasis engaging the imagination of the congregation.
  - Note whether actors can be heard:
    - without a microphone – they may need practice at projecting their voice
    - with radio microphones
    - from fixed microphones. Narration from one spot can be very effective accompanying mime; it can be used to allow the congregation to hear the thoughts of the character.
- Writing needs to bear in mind the potential actors.
  - What skills are available?
    - Write scripts that the actors will be happy to perform. Anxious actors produce anxious congregations who become embarrassed or concerned. Long scripts may be impractical, as most people are worried by lines to learn. Movement can help people remember what they are supposed to be saying.
  - How many actors?
    - With one or two actors, narration, mime or dialogue are still possible.
    - Mixed ages can bring something special to a drama, through the co-operation across boundaries.
- Sometimes working out ideas together can generate the script. Equally, sometimes ideas, words and actions need to be changed or developed.
- Check that the last words or actions leave the congregation at the right point for the next item in the order of service.

Taking time

- Allow time for a service to develop. (In the space of a few days after a planning meeting new ideas may emerge or the possibility of simplifying the original plan may become apparent. But you will need to check back with those involved to see what they think.)
- Push an idea around.
- Run the service through in your mind before God.
- Give yourself permission to change your mind.
- Give your group permission to change its mind.

Getting involved

The wise men, when they saw Jesus, bowed down, worshipped and presented gifts to him. They were not content with recognizing and honouring him in their minds, but followed that up with actions. In giving people the chance to do something, we widen the opportunities for them to worship. Doing is also a good form of learning since we remember more of what we do than of what we see or hear; and sharing actions can draw us closer together.

Symbolic actions have been used by the church throughout its history. There were the sacrifices and offerings of Old Testament worship and the teaching aids used by Jeremiah under God's instruction (e.g. Jeremiah 13, 19). At the Last Supper Jesus washed his disciples' feet and broke bread to share with them, and since the earliest days of the church, Christians have been baptized. All of these were actions that had symbolic meaning.

I used to think that symbols obscured the real truth and were, therefore, to be avoided. In fact, the opposite is true, because they speak to more than the intellect – opening understanding to all, and deepening our insights. Finding ways in which people can participate with an action makes the message personal to them.

One Good Friday, at the corner of the service sheet, there was a drawing of a thorny twig. After hearing the words 'God shows his love for us in

this: while we were yet sinners Christ died for us', people were invited, as an act of confession, to tear off that corner as a reminder of those things that they wanted to say sorry for. Following the promise of forgiveness ('If we confess our sins, God is faithful and just and will forgive us our sins and cleanse us from all unrighteousness') they were invited to leave their corner of paper with its thorn drawing at the foot of a cross. It was a very difficult thing to do.

The following Easter day, there were flowers where the thorns had been placed.

Symbolic actions that allow a personal response

Curling up for confession.

Uncurling for absolution.

Collecting a card in realization of God's presence.

Slotting an individually coloured bird into hands – 'God cares for you'.

Placing footprints beside prints representing those of Jesus. His footprints led up the church before the service and were turned round during a hymn to lead outside.

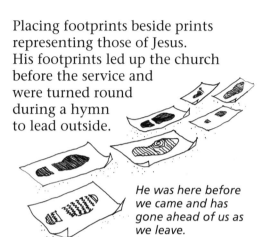

He was here before we came and has gone ahead of us as we leave.

Symbolic actions can also emphasize the oneness of the church. Individual symbols can be brought together to make a whole or people can become aware of sharing the same symbolic action.

Symbolic actions that emphasize the church as a whole

At the end of a Good Friday service, walking together through a doorway representing our access to God.

Making a pipe cleaner figure of oneself and placing it with others along a clay path, representing the journey we share.

But actions can divide

Choosing symbolic actions to use requires sensitivity to your own congregation. What would be welcome in one place might leave people squirming in another. Asking children to do something that adults are not happy to participate in is counter-productive. It leaves children feeling embarrassed and devalued.

When Jesus told parables, he was using symbols – they were so easily recognized that they invited listeners to join in the story in their imagination. In a similar way, seeing and doing sometimes helps our understanding.

Symbols that shed new light on teaching

A pile of cards about harvest. It is more effective to share out this pile of cards, giving one to each person, than simply to talk about there being enough food in the world for all.

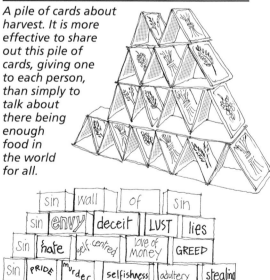

A wall of boxes, built up to show how sin separates us from God. OHP scenes of the first Good Friday were projected on to this wall, before it cracked. On Easter Day the wall had broken down.

Involvement in prayer

How can we involve everyone in praying?

As part of a service that aimed to inform people of different areas of ministry within the parish, a large street map was made. After models of key buildings had been constructed and added and we had prayed corporately for the parish, photocopies of a drawing of praying hands, distributed earlier, were collected from everyone and scattered over the map. The possibility of effective prayer suddenly seemed more real.

The map came out again a few years later when groups of people (according to where they were sitting) were given a piece of map and a photo of a key building in that area – school, pub, housing, day centre – with a little information to help them, and were then asked to pray together about it. The pieces of map were then placed together and the photos added.

Pictures and actions can help people pray who find words difficult to read or say. For example:

- Drawings of parts of God's creation can be held up as a silent prayer of thanksgiving or commitment to caring.
- Crumpled drawings can be used as a focus for confession and smoothed out after hearing words of absolution.
- Hands can be cupped to offer to God our sin for confession and

then wiped against each other, as if wiping them clean, the deaf and dumb language sign for forgiveness.
- Names or drawings of people to pray for can be written or drawn on slips of paper. They can then be collected, placed somewhere appropriate or held by the service leader and a prayer said asking God to hold the people named on them in his care. It is important that in this situation, people know that their prayers are between them and God alone – the unseen papers can be burnt prayerfully later.
- Words or pictures can be chosen from newspapers and offered to God, allowing people to pray for situations where words fail.
- Candles may be lit as the dark situations are mentioned alongside a refrain that asks for God to bring light.

Communion services

Communion services are opportunities for the whole church to come together in an act of worship that is rich in symbolism. In actual practice, the words said, the books or orders of service used, and the length of time the service takes can all be barriers to everyone feeling involved. It is worth considering what it would be like to be six years old, and to have come with your parents to a communion service. What would you see, hear, understand and feel? How would you feel if you had no church background but had become a regular and enthusiastic eleven-year-old member of the young people's group of the church?

The amount of involvement in a communion service can be increased if:

- opportunities are given for people to join in with short spoken phrases or songs
- there are visual images to help understanding – pictures on a screen; figures of the disciples at the Last Supper; drawings on an order of service
- orders of service contain only the words that are necessary and not everything that the minister will say – if they do, they can look as daunting as a prayer book
- prayers chosen are short with words that are easy to understand
- there are opportunities for children to learn about the Last Supper both in their own peer group teaching and occasionally in the context of a communion service. Acting out a eucharistic prayer can be very effective, for adults as well as children: actors can mime Jesus and the disciples at supper, Judas leaving the scene, bread being broken and wine being poured
- when children come up to receive a blessing rather than bread and wine the prayer should be said with sincerity and love – there are no second-class citizens in heaven
- communion is not seen as a separate entity from the rest of the service. If children come back into church to join the adults at the beginning of communion, it will help them and the adults if the children know why they are coming back and do not feel frustrated at having to leave the paint and fun behind. If communion is part of a whole all-age service it is good to look at the flow of the complete service – sometimes it will be best to have some teaching or praying after communion rather than before.

Some of these ideas involve a lot of thought and work, e.g. cutting cards and building doorways. But there are simple actions that do not require vast amounts of preparation, e.g. kneeling, standing up, greeting each other, moving forward or together, curling up for confession and unwinding for absolution. Good preparation demonstrates our desire to give our best to God, but it probably means that someone has stayed up very late! It is best achieved by a team of people. They will probably enjoy working together, and new friendships may be formed as well.

Becoming more involved in services is part of a learning process, not something that a service leader or planner can suddenly switch on. The symbols or actions we use need to fit happily into the whole act of worship and be offered to the congregation as opportunities. They need to be activities that:

- do not cause embarrassment
- are fully explained
- allow people to feel that it is all right not to participate
- allow people to participate at their own level.

Symbolic actions such as these can then become useful vehicles for our learning, our worship and our growing together.

ACTION

AIM: To consider the most appropriate ways in which people can get involved.

1. Consider how your congregation would respond to the suggestions in the box below. Fill in the cloud shapes for different age groups, then decide whether there would be a place for that suggestion or something similar in your church.

2. In your next service planning, highlight points where the congregation is invited to make a response – include words, songs, prayers and actions. Are there places where they could be more involved?

How would your own congregation feel if they were invited to join in these actions? (Different age groups may respond in different ways.)

	Feelings	Is there a place for it? Yes/no/not likely/possibly
Singing 'My God is so big' with actions.		
Curling up for a confession.		
Stretching out for the absolution.		
Making a pipe cleaner model of themselves, and adding it to a group representing people on their way to God.		
In groups, putting a puzzle together.		
Laying a picture of a fingerprint on a tray, as a sign of thankfulness for the touch of God on their lives.		

Coping with criticism

Planning and running all-age worship services is a creative process, which may well break new ground. As such it is likely to be open to misunderstanding and criticism in a way that even a badly run traditional service is not. Creativity demands that we give something of ourselves in the process. If we are involved in all-age worship, we are probably passionately concerned that the whole church does worship together. So criticism when it comes is bound to hurt. It digs into our desire to provide what we feel the church needs and it cuts slashes in our creativity. Yet its digging and cutting may be a necessary tool in the cultivating of an all-age worship plant. Perhaps it can be used as part of the divine pruning process of John 14.

So how do we cope? And can we even turn it to our positive advantage? Here are some ideals:

- Separate yourself from what is being criticized.
- Accept that God loves both you and the critics.
- Get things in perspective.
- Look at specifics.
- Act, where necessary.
- Work with a group.

An example

It is not a good idea to dwell on criticism just after a service. At that time you are vulnerable and probably tired. Read Clarence's letter (page 38). If you had received this letter you might deduce that you had failed to cater for his emotional and spiritual needs and therefore you have failed in your service aims.

Alternatively, you might screw the letter up and toss it away, saying: 'Clarence never did get on with his relations, and that incident with the dramatic society has left him even more touchy, but he doesn't have to take it out on me.'

Both reactions take the letter too personally and miss out on what might need to be learnt from it.

Specifics

So read Clarence's letter carefully and, remembering that God's love for Clarence with all his shortcomings is as great as his love for you with all yours, look at the specific points about the family worship service. In among the machine-gun spray of his criticism are the following points:

- too short
- too noisy
- too childish
- no teaching
- inaudible drama
- for entertainment only.

All of these need to be considered, as Clarence might possibly be making some valid points. With a set of principles, like the roots from which we began, it is easier to recognize which criticisms are just. For example, if you decide that Clarence is right and that the service was pure entertainment, then you would have to agree with him that this was not appropriate, since the service cannot have been God-centred. On the other hand, if you feel that the service was short because the needs of the younger children whose attention

span is very short had been taken into account, then you would be able to explain this to him and not feel bound to make services longer.

So, bearing in mind your roots and taking a look at the service, preferably with a group, you can come to some decisions. If you work in a group, you should be able to discuss the problems without losing your vision or disappearing down the spiral of feeling a failure. Together you are better able to find positive solutions where necessary.

Having digested the criticism you need to:

- take note of the points for improvement (in this case perhaps audibility and more attention given to the needs of adults)
- communicate with the critics (Clarence has asked to see you!)

- keep people informed (Clarence's letter suggests little understanding of the aim of all-age worship – perhaps this needs to be worked at).

The positive side

If the all-age worship group/person is a listener, then by listening they will have contributed to the reservoir of trust within the church. Criticism can be a useful tool in the refining of what we do. It can also be devastatingly painful, but you have a choice in what you do with that pain. Aim to bring it to God and then view the situation with him. He, after all, has the overall view. What you do in planning and leading services is like a jigsaw piece within his whole picture.

ACTION

AIM: To practise dealing with criticism, so that it is easier to react rightly to the real thing.

Using a copy of Clarence's letter:

- highlight the points that you feel should be considered by the group that designed the service at Clarence's church
- consider which of these points could be improved
- list the things that you would want to say to Clarence
- decide what would need to be conveyed to those taking part
- discuss how you would do it
- consider how a church planning team can try to ensure that the aims of the all-age worship services are better understood by the congregation.

Dear Vicar,

I have wrestled regarding whether or not to write and send this letter, particularly in the aftermath of my recent misfortune, the details of which I presume you are unaware as I have not received a visit from you. As much as it grieves me, I feel that some things are better said than not said, especially when the well-being of the church is at stake, and so I write to you concerning last Sunday's 10 o'clock family service.

Firstly, had I arrived any later than I did, owing to unforeseen circumstances that I cannot divulge, I might just as well not have bothered attending the service at all. It was all over within forty minutes, leaving me to entertain a sister-in-law with a difficult temperament until 1 o'clock when the lunch was ready. I had in my mind calculated that I would not get away from church until 12.30, leaving only 20 minutes with her on arriving home which would be relatively easy to fill.

The service, in addition to being too short, was also too noisy, too childish and contained no teaching of any real substance to spiritually nourish those of us in attendance. I myself left as empty as I had arrived, which says much about the quality of service provided for us.

As for the drama, performed by the young people and whose voices were almost inaudible, may I say that had I desired entertainment of that sort I would have bought tickets for the circus. As you will know from our previous telephone conversations, my painful rebuff by the local amateur dramatic society has left me quite unable to tolerate egocentric theatrical indulgence in any form, and so to be presented with it in church was unbearable.

I must stress that this letter is written in love and for the purpose of building up the body. I appreciate that we do have a large number of young people in the congregation and that their interests are vastly different from mine. However, we must be careful not to pander to their whims and fancies. I believe that young people are the church of tomorrow and as such they should wait their turn, while we, the church of today, receive services that we enjoy and that suit our needs.

I do hope that this letter finds you well, Vicar, and I look forward to seeing you soon. I am at home every afternoon these days.

Yours sincerely

Clarence Grace

Clarence Grace

A long hot summer?

Summertime brings the prospect of a rest, or a change, or excitement, or catching up with friends... Viewed by the church mouse or church pigeon (or whoever stays in residence) the summer holidays make up a different picture. There is more than the usual coming and going, congregations fluctuate, children disappear with excitement, their leaders take a break, decisions are left until September. So how would those who are present on any Sunday in the summer complete a postcard to send to one of their absent friends?

'Rain is non-stop but wish you were here for these summer Sundays. The church has been...'

or

'Marvellous sunshine, but we are missing you and the rest. It has been hard not having our usual Sunday diet. Looking forward to seeing you and to September.'

Summer can be a time of problems and opportunities. We can choose to ignore it, or take the bull by the horns, grapple with the problems and grasp the opportunities.

Problems and opportunities

When we started to take a look at the summer period, we saw that several problems arose for us from having seven all-age services to span the school holidays.

- Children had less freedom; they were always with their parents and not their peers.

- Adults missed having some adult sermons.
- Holidays made continuity difficult to achieve for those leading the services, both in their own minds and for the congregation.
- Each service needed to be able to stand by itself.

After several years of working on the summer series of services, we saw that the opportunities that the summer gives us are:

- a chance to do something different from the usual
- being able to look at subjects from a new angle
- the possibility of introducing new input into worship
- time for small groups to work together on a challenge, often with people they would not normally be with.

There were two main solutions for our set of problems listed above.

1. We decided to plan a seven-week programme that included workshops on some Sundays.
2. We devised built-in continuity features for the services.

1. Workshops

Workshops are opportunities to tackle some activities related to the day's teaching and worship. They might include painting, model-making, cooking, woodwork, percussion-playing, drama... They are designed to feed back into the rest of the service on the same day or to provide material for subsequent Sundays. Being open to everyone means that workshops must provide

CHAPTER 9

for a range of skills. It also means that members of the congregation have the opportunity to work with people other than their peers. What is done in a workshop depends on the space, resources and skills available and the imagination and ingenuity of the planners.

The existence of workshops alongside sermons gives everybody the opportunity to increase their understanding of the topic either by hearing a sermon or by participating in the activities of the workshop.

Depending on the staff available and the topic chosen, the seven-week programme has usually contained four all-age services and three workshop/sermon services.

Some examples:

● For a series on Paul's second missionary journey, a relief map of the Mediterranean coastal lands was made in a workshop. It was used to track Paul's progress on subsequent Sundays.
● A small percussion group with people of all ages prepared music for songs used at the end of one service.
● 'Babylon' with street market, hanging gardens and stencilled archway was rapidly constructed in the church hall. Following the sermon everyone met up in Babylon to feel its foreignness, listen to Psalm 137, confess and return.

2. Continuity features

When the subject has been chosen, continuity features sometimes suggest themselves. Having decided on the exile and realized that a number of quite distinct characters would be involved – Cyrus, Ezra, Nebuchadnezzar, etc. – we thought of masks, then of waxworks, and finally opted for costume models as in a museum. They were fun to dress but difficult to move about; we managed

---

Workshops presented as a challenge seem to have an appeal.

1. People need to know something about what they are doing – 'When the Israelites were taken to Babylon they would have found it very different because…'
2. People need to see the point of what they are doing – 'When the adults join us we want this hall to be transformed so that they can experience how it might have felt to have been taken to Babylon.'
3. People need some space for their own creativity within frameworks that ensure that something will have been achieved.
4. The task needs to be bigger or more fun or more difficult than children tackle on a normal Sunday.
5. People need to be given a task that seems slightly impossible – 'You have twenty minutes to do it!'

to borrow shop-window mannequins but not their stands, so as they were heaved out of the way for weddings and other services, limbs tended to fall off. The fun and challenge of turning leggy Western girls into ancient Middle-Eastern kings made coping with their loosely fitted legs worthwhile!

From the museum models came the idea for a museum curator to be the narrator for the series, setting the scene and describing the character and his actions. When the curator was unavailable, an assistant took his place. Continuity was therefore provided visually by the growing line-up of models and in the content of the services by the curator's talk.

Techniques that work well can be adapted and used again in other years, while some are best quietly dropped.

Suggestions for continuity features are:

- a relief map with a model moved to track a journey – this is fun to make, but not very enthralling afterwards
- OHP 'picture postcards' of places visited – this can be prepared in advance
- same storyteller – but this makes a lot of work for one person
- a 'pathway of pictures' for a character study – the pieces can be prepared in a workshop
- newspaper reports following events – this allows for different reporters, so the workload is shared
- diary excerpts – these can be written and/or read by different people

- a huge picturebook made up of pages matching diary entries – this can be prepared in advance.

Perhaps the ideal links are those suggested by the subject matter, which can be executed by a number of people in advance and then assembled or performed with ease throughout the series.

A different slant

The subject for the summer series has to be able to be divided into the right number of episodes, with enough in each for it to stand by itself. Taking a long-term view of events is something not always possible during the year; this generates a piecemeal approach to the Bible and its teaching. A seven-week span, however, enables a sweep of history to be taken in, e.g. the Israelites in exile, or from Egypt to Jericho.

Sometimes a different viewpoint throws new light on well-known events. For example:

1. The apostle John's growing perception of Jesus, as seen through his own eyes, allows people to look at their own perceptions and growth.
2. Looking at the life of David as a pathway (in which he was seen moving both towards and away from God as his story unfolded), is encouraging; even David did not progress smoothly and quickly in his understanding and obedience to God. (He fought in the name of the Lord against Goliath, lied to the priest at Nob, trusted God, killed Uriah for Bathsheba, before repenting...)

CHAPTER 9

One summer's programme

The current interest in Celtic Christianity gave rise to a series based on John's Gospel – the Gospel that had most influenced the early Celtic Christians. In it we followed John as he watched and listened to Jesus, from the time that they first met until after the first Easter. It set out to consider how John came to see Jesus as Creator, as the one who offered eternal life, and as God. The series included adult sermons, workshops and worship with a Celtic feel.

During the series there were short readings from John's diary – various invited people had taken the Bible passage and retold it as if they were John writing his diary at the end of the day, e.g. on the evening after he had given up fishing and started following Jesus. A giant picture book was opened to reveal a picture of the same event.

In the first workshop people were shown a slide of a Celtic cross with its carved Gospel scenes and patterns

and animals round the circular section. Then they were asked to help make a huge cardboard cross with scenes from each week's story. The sections were cut out beforehand so that each scene could be depicted separately by sticking on card, sticks, string and netting. Later it was painted with grey emulsion paint so that it resembled stone.

As a final reminder of the series, each person was given a small Celtic cross made from card. It was made in two parts, the cross being photocopied and cut out beforehand and the circle decorated with fingerprint animals in a workshop.

The skeleton programme (opposite) shows how the workshops (shaded) fed into the rest of the services.

The summer series has been fun to plan and has solved the problems we were facing. It has opened up opportunities that do not seem to be there at other times of the year. It needs at least one person with a vision to make it work, preferably a group of people so that ideas and responsibility can be shared. Then as many others as possible are needed to carry it out.

TITLE	ITEMS IN SERVICE
1. MEETING JESUS Mark 1:19,20	Introduction to the series First entry in John's diary with picture of Galilean boats in the giant picture book Responsive Celtic liturgy

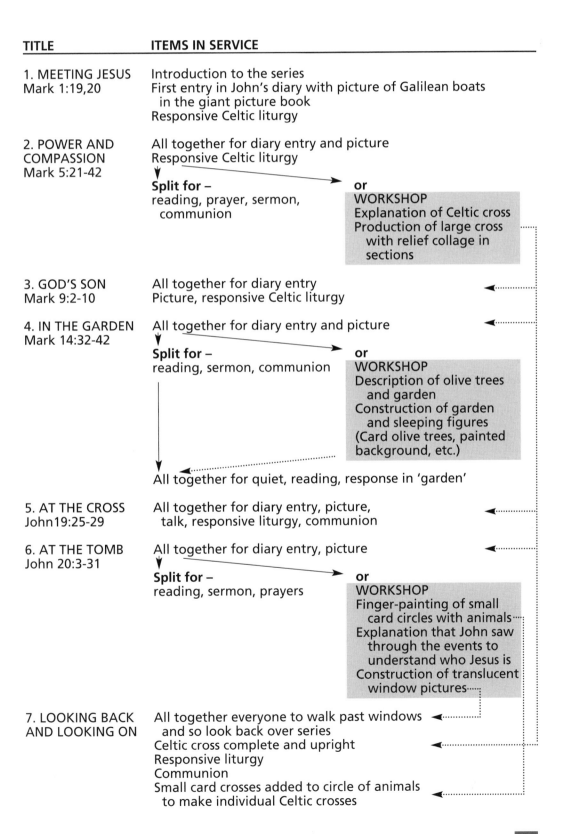

2. POWER AND COMPASSION
Mark 5:21-42

All together for diary entry and picture
Responsive Celtic liturgy

Split for –
reading, prayer, sermon, communion

or

WORKSHOP
Explanation of Celtic cross
Production of large cross
with relief collage in
sections

3. GOD'S SON
Mark 9:2-10

All together for diary entry
Picture, responsive Celtic liturgy

4. IN THE GARDEN
Mark 14:32-42

All together for diary entry and picture

Split for –
reading, sermon, communion

or

WORKSHOP
Description of olive trees
and garden
Construction of garden
and sleeping figures
(Card olive trees, painted
background, etc.)

All together for quiet, reading, response in 'garden'

5. AT THE CROSS
John 19:25-29

All together for diary entry, picture,
talk, responsive liturgy, communion

6. AT THE TOMB
John 20:3-31

All together for diary entry, picture

Split for –
reading, sermon, prayers

or

WORKSHOP
Finger-painting of small
card circles with animals
Explanation that John saw
through the events to
understand who Jesus is
Construction of translucent
window pictures

**7. LOOKING BACK
AND LOOKING ON**

All together everyone to walk past windows
and so look back over series
Celtic cross complete and upright
Responsive liturgy
Communion
Small card crosses added to circle of animals
to make individual Celtic crosses

AIM: To look at summer in your church to see if there are problems to be tackled or opportunities to be taken.

1. The problems you face during the summer may be quite different to the ones described here, but visualizing summer at your church through the eyes of different people may enable you to discover new opportunities. Using copies of Worksheet H, complete the postcards as if they were being sent from different groups within your church to their friends away on holiday. If you are not sure what people would say, ask them what they appreciate or find difficult about church in the summer.

2. Discuss your answers to question 1 and see if they suggest a way forward.

3. If you think that it would be good to produce a linked programme of services, work through the 'Holiday planning' flow chart below.

Holiday planning

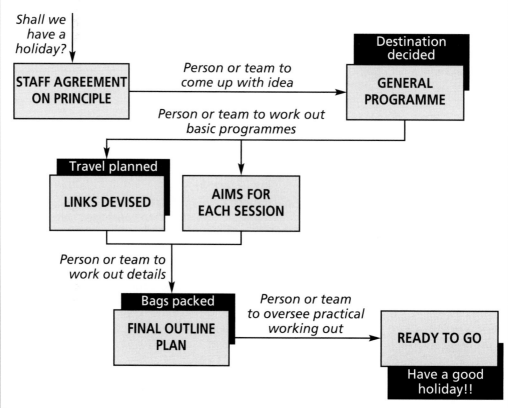

Shall we have a holiday?

STAFF AGREEMENT ON PRINCIPLE

Person or team to come up with idea

Destination decided — GENERAL PROGRAMME

Person or team to work out basic programmes

Travel planned — LINKS DEVISED

AIMS FOR EACH SESSION

Person or team to work out details

Bags packed — FINAL OUTLINE PLAN

Person or team to oversee practical working out

READY TO GO

Have a good holiday!!

The problems: **The opportunities**

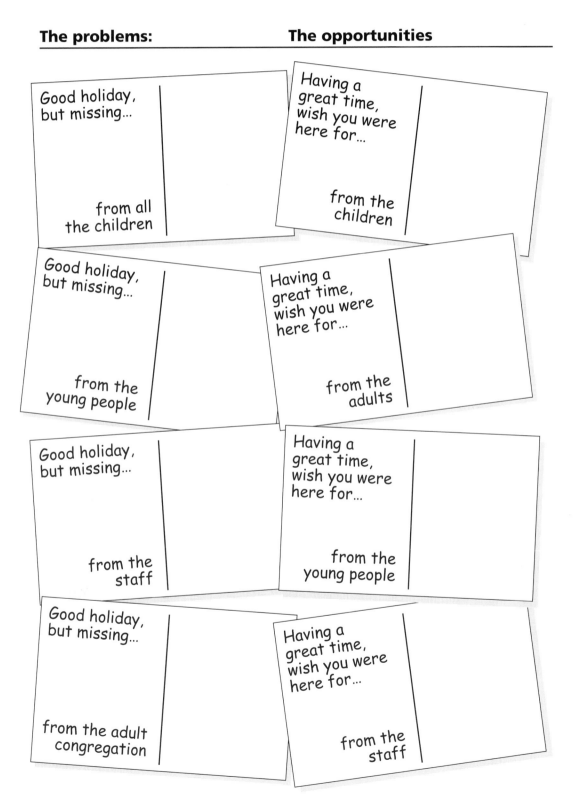

Good holiday,
but missing...

from all
the children

Having a
great time,
wish you were
here for...

from the
children

Good holiday,
but missing...

from the
young people

Having a
great time,
wish you were
here for...

from the
adults

Good holiday,
but missing...

from the
staff

Having a
great time,
wish you were
here for...

from the
young people

Good holiday,
but missing...

from the adult
congregation

Having a
great time,
wish you were
here for...

from the
staff

The garden

Lucy's story

Lucy stood at the door of the church. It was raining outside and the service had ended fifteen minutes ago. She stood beside her mother and waited. Her mother was talking to old Mrs Foster and the conversation droned on.

Lucy looked down at her shoes. The scabs on her legs were itching dreadfully, but she knew that levering them off would make her knees bleed again. They had bled a lot when she fell over and she couldn't remember anything that had hurt so much. Their class had been allowed out for playtime at lunch after a morning of rain and it was a vicious push from Rebecca that had sent her skidding across the asphalt. At church they sometimes prayed for people who were ill. The vicar had prayed for Mr Smedley's gout this morning. Lucy wondered what gout was and if it hurt as much as her knees had last Thursday. Perhaps you could pray for some pain, but not for others.

Mrs Foster tapped Lucy on the shoulder.

'I did enjoy your little play in the service last week,' she said. 'You did your piece beautifully – I could hear every word.' She turned back to Lucy's mother. 'So nice for the children to be involved.'

Lucy considered whether or not Mrs Foster had remembered what she had said in the play. Lucy had been the innkeeper and she had liked saying that Mary and Joseph were special. It was an important line and Lucy was sure that they had been special. After all, Jesus was special, even when he was a tiny baby.

The service had been okay, they usually were. But afterwards was a bore. Why do adults always have to drink coffee? Lucy wished that they would go, she wanted to be at home so she could look at her new hamster to see if he was still asleep. It had been fun choosing him last week. She knew that she had chosen right, she had never seen such a silky, silvery one before. Mrs Foster was going on about her nephew. Lucy had heard all about William. Every time Mrs Foster came round for coffee, she went on about clever William.

Lucy looked out again at the rain splashing on the church step.

'Come along then, Lucy,' said her mother, extracting herself from the conversation. 'We must get a move on. Did you have a good time this morning?'

Lucy stepped out into the rain and looked up at her mother. 'Mum,' she said, 'will there be children in heaven?'

A community together

Lucy's church had gone a long way in providing opportunities for her involvement, but still Lucy felt that there was something lacking in its community life.

Developing the church as a community may be beyond the duties of an all-age worship-planning group, but the group needs to be aware of its importance. There may be:

- events that could be suggested
- attitudes that could be cultivated
- ways that the needs and gifts of the children and young people could be brought to the attention of the adults
- and vice versa.

Sometimes a slight change made to the plans for an event can make the difference between children feeling wanted and feeling rejected or bored. For example, have they got something to do while adults are talking over a meal? Is there something in a display/production that will interest both young and old and that they can talk about together?

As the church becomes more of a community where every member is valued, it becomes a place of trust where:

- the foundations of trust in God can be built
- stories of faith can be learnt from people that are trusted
- doubts and questions can be raised without fear of disgrace
- everyone feels accepted with their own struggles, interests and gifts, and has the support in prayer and love that they need.

ACTION

AIM: To consider if there are ways in which the community life of your church could be improved.

1. Listen to Lucy's story (on the previous page) and decide in what ways her church had tried to make her feel involved.

   How do you think Mrs Foster made Lucy feel?

   How could a greater sense of community be encouraged in Lucy's church?

2. How could a greater sense of community be encouraged in your church? Brainstorm some ideas, then pray over the possibilities looking to see what, if anything, you should do as individuals or as a group.

CHAPTER 10

Into that community children and young adults will bring their own gifts:

- their faith, with its emphasis on trust and action, reminding adults that God can be trusted completely and that faith without action is dead
- their ability to smell insincerity from a distance, encouraging adults to perceive their own hypocrisy and double standards
- their wonder, hope, energy and imagination, inspiring adults to move beyond a cerebral faith
- their open love and care that ignores the boundaries and difficulties that adults tend to see.

The presence of children and young adults is good for us all.

Finally

If we begin to doubt the wisdom of spending so much time in preparation, rehearsal, on the phone involving people, then we need to be reminded that just one person's communication with God is of infinite value. If we are able to provide opportunities for our church as a community to speak with God, we have been given an enormous privilege and every scrap of effort is more than worthwhile.

They came out together, carrying the huge card between them. All of the under-elevens had spent most of the morning adding animals, birds, plants and elements of weather to it. It was a wild collection of parrots and snowflakes, guinea pigs and gorillas.

Joe had made a whale. He had been keen on them since he had seen a television programme on whaling. He had been shocked to see the whale slowly dying. But his whale on the picture had been rising from the sea and spouting a great plume of paper water droplets. He had been pleased with it.

Joe had helped to carry the card into the church and set it carefully down. Someone had read something about God creating the sea, teeming with creatures beyond number – living things both large and small. Jack had switched the light on so that it shone out through letters cut in the card: G O D. 'God must care about the whales,' Joe thought.

Joe looked across at his leader, carrying the other end of the card. 'It was good what we did this morning,' he said.